Searchlight BOOKS™

Climate Change

Climate Change and

Extreme Storms

Mary Dykstra

Lerner Publications ◆ Minneapolis

To the hardworking scientists
around the world

Lerner Publications Company
A division of Lerner Publishing Group, Inc.
241 First Avenue North
Minneapolis, MN 55401 USA

For reading levels and more information, look up this title
at www.lernerbooks.com.

Main body text set in Adrianna Regular 14/20.
Typeface provided by Chank.

Library of Congress Cataloging-in-Publication Data

Names: Dykstra, Mary, 1952– author.
Title: Climate change and extreme storms / Mary Dykstra.
Description: Minneapolis : Lerner Publications, 2019. | Series: Searchlight books.
    Climate change | Includes bibliographical references and index. | Audience: Age 8–11. |
    Audience: Grade 4 to 6.
Identifiers: LCCN 2018011473 (print) | LCCN 2018015419 (ebook) | ISBN 9781541543669
    (eb pdf) | ISBN 9781541538634 (lb : alk. paper)
Subjects: LCSH: Climatic changes—Juvenile literature. | Severe storms—Juvenile literature.
Classification: LCC QC903.15 (ebook) | LCC QC903.15 .D95 2019 (print) |
    DDC 551.55—dc23

LC record available at https://lccn.loc.gov/2018011473

Manufactured in the United States of America
1-45046-35873-5/22/2018

Contents

Chapter 1

OUR CLIMATE IS CHANGING . . . 4

Chapter 2

HURRICANES AND OTHER TROPICAL STORMS . . . 9

Chapter 3

TORNADOES, HAILSTORMS, AND MORE . . . 15

Chapter 4

LOOKING FOR SOLUTIONS . . . 22

What You Can Do • 28
Climate Change Timeline • 29
Glossary • 30
Learn More about Extreme Storms • 31
Index • 32

OUR CLIMATE IS CHANGING

Extreme storms get our attention. Howling winds rip off roofs and knock down buildings. Heavy rainfall floods entire neighborhoods. Blizzards bring so much snow that schools close for days. These weather events are especially large and dangerous. And they are happening more often because of climate change.

Hurricanes are happening more frequently than in the past.

Hurricane Irma in 2017 caused lots of damage. Many homes and buildings were destroyed by strong winds and flooding.

Weather is what happens in the atmosphere around us every day. Climate is the average weather in a place over many years. The weather where you live might be cool and rainy today, even though you live in a climate that is warm and dry.

Recent weather events worry many scientists. Strong storms are happening more often. Some are causing record damage. In 2017, sixteen US weather events cost more than $1 billion each.

Cooking Up Storms

Earth's air and oceans are getting hotter. This temperature change is happening faster than in the past. Seventeen of the last eighteen years have been the warmest on record. Ocean temperatures have gone up too—about 1.5°F (0.8°C) since 1901.

The gasoline used to power cars is a fossil fuel. Using fossil fuels contributes to the temperature changes scientists are seeing.

More extreme snowstorms are connected to warmer ocean temperatures. Evaporating ocean water leads to more moisture for storms all over the world.

These changes might not seem significant, yet they are indeed. As the ocean gets warmer, more water evaporates. This results in more clouds. The clouds bring more rain and storms. Even if you live far from the coast, the ocean affects your weather. That's because the ocean temperature plays a big part in where and when storms occur.

Rising Seas

As temperatures rise, glaciers melt faster. The melting ice causes sea levels to go up. As water warms, it expands, or gets bigger. This also causes a rise in sea levels. Many cities along the US Atlantic and Gulf coasts are less than 10 feet (3 m) above sea level. They are at risk during storms that bring heavy rain and high wind. The strong wind can push the ocean water onto land in what is called storm surge.

Warming air temperatures are melting glaciers around the world. This ice adds to the sea level as it melts.

Chapter 2

HURRICANES AND OTHER TROPICAL STORMS

Hurricanes are tropical storms that form over the Atlantic Ocean. These huge storms have damaging winds of 74 miles (119 km) an hour or more. Hurricanes form when warm air rising from the ocean meets colder air above, forming clouds. The winds get stronger as the storms move over the warm ocean waters toward land. These storms are called typhoons or cyclones in other parts of the world.

At the center of this hurricane is the storm's eye. This area experiences calmer weather than other areas touched by the storm.

Scientists assign hurricanes numbers based on wind speed. A higher number indicates a more extreme storm. A Category 5 hurricane is the most dangerous. It has winds of 157 miles (253 km) an hour or more.

STRONG WINDS FROM HURRICANES CAN UPROOT TREES AND BLOW ROOFS OFF BUILDINGS.

Hurricane Maria brought heavy downpours, strong winds, and flooding to Puerto Rico, causing massive damage to the island.

Recently, the Atlantic region had three rare Category 5 hurricanes in back-to-back years. Matthew hit Haiti in the Caribbean in 2016. This storm caused lots of damage before moving north along the US coast. Hurricanes Irma and Maria struck the following year. They traveled farther than any other Category 5 hurricanes in history. Puerto Rico was especially hard hit by Maria. Many homes were without roofs or power for months after the storm.

Hurricanes Katrina and Harvey

Hurricane Katrina first came to shore in Florida in 2005. The hurricane dumped heavy rain and damaged many buildings because of its high winds. Katrina then went back over the Gulf of Mexico and gained strength. It came back to shore in Louisiana, Mississippi, and Alabama. The storm surge was higher than a two-story house in some places.

These homes in New Orleans remained underwater after the storm surge from Katrina flooded the low-lying city.

MANY PEOPLE HAD TO ABANDON THEIR
PROPERTY WHEN HARVEY'S STORM SURGE AND
RAINFALL CAUSED SIGNIFICANT FLOODING.

Harvey was a Category 4 hurricane that hit Texas in 2017. Many storms move on quickly, but Harvey stayed in the area for days. Parts of Houston got up to 50 inches (127 cm) of rainfall in a week. Many people lost their homes because of flooding and wind damage. The storm damaged or destroyed about one million cars.

STEM In Depth: Storms Affect Wildlife Too

Hurricane Harvey hit Texas in August 2017. At that time of the year, most whooping cranes in the wild were in Canada, but scientists knew that these endangered birds soon would return to Texas for the winter. Harvey pushed salty ocean water inland to ponds where the cranes would eat and drink. So scientists used pumps to replace the salt water with the fresh water that cranes need to survive. Scientists will continue to watch the birds to see how they are doing.

Chapter 3

TORNADOES, HAILSTORMS, AND MORE

Climate change also may be causing an increase in other types of severe storms. Tornadoes are spinning columns of air that form during thunderstorms. They develop when hot air from the ground rises and meets cooler air above. The United States has more tornadoes each year than any other country. Many occur in an area in the south-central United States known as Tornado Alley. Cold air from Canada comes down and mixes with hot air in this region, making tornadoes more likely.

This tornado in Kansas formed during a thunderstorm. Kansas is in Tornado Alley.

Scientists who study storms use radar to track tornadoes. They look at how storms form so they can try to predict their impact.

Some tornadoes have wind speeds of 300 miles (483 km) an hour or more. Tornadoes can level entire towns or neighborhoods in their paths. In the past, some strong tornadoes killed hundreds of people. These days, meteorologists use radar to predict when and where a tornado might touch down. Warning systems such as sirens and alerts save lives. They help people know when to find shelter.

Harmful Hail

Thunderstorms also can bring hail, lightning, and heavy rain. Hail forms when drops of water freeze together in the cold upper part of clouds. A hailstone that weighed almost 2 pounds (0.9 kg) fell in South Dakota in 2010. It was almost as big as a soccer ball! Large hailstones can dent cars, break windows, and flatten crops. In 2017, a hailstorm in Colorado caused more than $1 billion in damage.

This hail may seem small, but it can damage property and crops, costing a lot of money.

IN DECEMBER 2017, A SNOWSTORM HIT ERIE, PENNSYLVANIA. IT DROPPED MORE THAN 5 FEET (1.5 M) OF SNOW IN THREE DAYS!

Snow Days

Snowstorms also can be dangerous. Extreme storms with heavy snow and high winds may be happening more often because of climate change. As the warm ocean waters evaporate, they feed more moisture into the snowstorms.

Blizzards are snowstorms with high winds of at least 35 miles (56.3 km) an hour. Blowing snow can make it very hard to see. It can be dangerous to travel during a blizzard.

Nor'easters are extreme storms that occur along the eastern coast of the United States. A nor'easter may bring heavy snow, rain, and strong winds. In 2018, four nor'easters struck in March. Scientists are looking at how climate change may be causing more of these storms.

Four nor'easter storms hit New York in March 2018. Some people used umbrellas to shield themselves from the blowing snow.

Drought and Wildfires

Scientists think that while some places are getting more rain and snow because of climate change, others are getting less. This may be caused in part by the warming of Earth and a related shift in wind patterns.

Water supply emergencies are becoming increasingly common in drier climates.

WATER LEVEL

Lake Of The Woods Mutual Water Co.
Water Emergency Please Restrict Use

Droughts happen when little or no rain falls over a long period. They can lead to wildfires, which can spread quickly as dry leaves and branches fuel the fire. If heavy rain falls after the fires, a mudslide can occur. In January 2018, a half inch (1.3 cm) of rain fell in Montecito, California, in just five minutes. The resulting mudslide destroyed more than one hundred homes and killed twenty-one people.

Wildfires in California in 2017 burned thousands of acres in the southern part of the state.

Chapter 4

LOOKING FOR SOLUTIONS

Meteorologists think we will get more extreme storms if climate change keeps up at the current rate. But many people are taking steps to help our planet and to prepare for those storms.

New types of satellites and tools are tracking hurricanes more closely. Scientists create computer models using data gathered by the satellites. These models help them predict when and where storms may occur. They then can warn people to get out of these areas before the storm hits.

Satellites in space take pictures of entire storms. The images help to track the strength and size of a storm.

STEM In Depth: Eye in the Sky

TIROS-1 was the world's first weather satellite. The United States sent it into space in 1960. The satellite carried two cameras and worked for only seventy-eight days. Modern weather satellites carry much better tools for measuring temperatures, wind speeds, and more. They can operate in orbit for ten or more years. They can share information with countries around the world, helping them prepare for storms.

Fighting Storm Surge

Engineers are looking at better ways to control storm surge and prevent flooding. A system of pump stations and gates was installed in New Orleans after Hurricane Katrina. Taller floodwalls were built to hold water back during storms.

Some places in Florida are trying a different approach. They want to be ready if sea levels keep rising and storms hit the area. They are raising the level of some roads in hopes that they will not be flooded.

Floodgates and pump stations prevent flooding after a storm by stopping storm surge from entering and pumping excess water out of a city.

Wetlands along the coast are an important part of the ecosystem. They provide food and shelter to many plants and animals.

In many US states, people are working to save coastal wetlands. Marshes and other wetlands act like sponges during storms, keeping areas from flooding. These valuable habitats also provide homes and food for birds and other wildlife. Some people are trying to pass laws that protect the wetlands from being drained and built upon. Groups are raising money to buy wetlands and keep them in their natural state.

Building Better Buildings

Many coastal areas now require better materials for new buildings. Builders install metal roofs with strong fasteners so the roofs won't blow off during storms. Many new homes have metal shutters to cover windows and keep them from breaking when high winds send objects flying.

Builders in coastal areas are using stronger materials to make sure that buildings can stand up to hurricane-force winds.

Fossil fuels bring electricity to many homes and buildings. Turning off the lights means using less fossil fuel.

We may not be able to change the weather, but we can prepare for it. And we can change the choices we make every day to help our planet. Some simple actions, such as turning off lights, may help slow down climate change. We can all be part of the solution!

What You Can Do

- **Check with your local animal shelter to see how you can help pets, nearby or far away, that have lost their homes due to storms.** Storms don't just hurt people. They affect pets too!

- **Find out more about the kinds of jobs that deal with extreme weather.** See if a science program or summer camp in your area can help you explore these careers.

- **Visit https://www.ready.gov/kids/build-a-kit for a storm checklist.** Put together a kit to use in an extreme storm. Your kit should include flashlights, water, and nutritious and nonperishable foods.

- **Donate clothing or food after a hurricane or other storm.** Contact your local Red Cross office to find out what people need and how to make a donation.

Climate Change Timeline

1900 A hurricane kills more than six thousand people in Galveston, Texas.

1925 The Tri-State Tornado roars through Missouri, Illinois, and Indiana on March 18, killing almost seven hundred people. Its winds were as high as 260 miles (418 km) an hour.

1953 The National Weather Service starts giving hurricanes female names. Male names were added in the late 1970s.

1970 The Bhola Cyclone kills up to half a million people in Southeast Asia. The storm surge floods low-lying islands, where many people live.

2005 Hurricane Katrina hits the southeastern United States in August, killing nearly two thousand people.

2017 Hurricanes Irma and Maria combined travel farther than any other Category 5 storms in an Atlantic hurricane season.

Glossary

atmosphere: the layer of air that surrounds Earth

blizzard: an extreme snowstorm with winds above 35 miles (56 km) an hour

climate: the typical weather for an area

drought: a long dry period when an area does not receive enough rain

evaporate: when heat causes liquid to turn into gas

glacier: a very large area of ice that moves slowly over land

meteorologist: a scientist who studies weather and Earth's atmosphere

mudslide: a large amount of mud that slides down a hill or mountain, sometimes following a heavy rainfall

storm surge: water pushed onto land by wind during a hurricane. It is measured by how much higher the water is than the normal tidal level.

weather satellite: a machine that orbits, or goes around, Earth and sends back information and photographs helpful in predicting storms

Learn More about Extreme Storms

Books

Kostigen, Thomas. *Extreme Weather: Surviving Tornadoes, Sandstorms, Hailstorms, Blizzards, Hurricanes, and More!* Washington, DC: National Geographic, 2014. Learn even more about climate change and preparing for extreme storms.

Kurtz, Kevin. *Climate Change and Rising Temperatures*. Minneapolis: Lerner Publications, 2019. Find out more about why Earth and its oceans are warming up.

Roker, Al. *Al Roker's Extreme Weather*. New York: HarperCollins, 2017. Explore a wide range of weather events with a well-known TV meteorologist.

Websites

Climate Kids
https://climatekids.nasa.gov
Learn about climate change and what we can do to help solve the problem.

A Student's Guide to Global Climate Change
https://www3.epa.gov/climatechange//kids/index.html
See the impacts of climate change around the world. See how you can think like a scientist.

Weather Science
http://youngmeteorologist.org/educator-resources/weather-science/
Review basic information about weather and extreme storms. Read about some of the tools meteorologists use to predict weather.

Index

atmosphere, 5

blizzards, 4, 19

droughts, 21

floods, 4, 13, 24–25

hail, 17
Hurricane Harvey, 13–14
Hurricane Katrina, 12, 24

mudslides, 21

satellites, 22, 23
storm surge, 8, 12, 24

thunderstorms, 15, 17
Tornado Alley, 15
tornadoes, 15–16

wetlands, 25
wildfires, 21

Photo Acknowledgments

Image credits: Warren Faidley/Corbis/Getty Images, p. 4; Chip Somodevilla/Getty Images, p. 5; Mongkol Chuewong/Moment/Getty Images, p. 6; Tainar/Shutterstock.com, p. 7; Mario Tama/Getty Images, p. 8; NASA/NOAA GOES Project/Getty Images, p. 9; Joe Raedle/Getty Images, p. 10; Mario Tama/Getty Images, p. 11; Yann Arthus-Bertrand/Getty Images, p. 12; Joe Raedle/Getty Images, p. 13; AP Photo/LM Otero, p. 14; Cultura Exclusive/Jason Persoff Stormdoctor/Getty Images, p. 15; Drew Angerer/Getty Images, p. 16; RStelmach/iStock/Getty Images, p. 17; AP Photo/Christopher Millette/Erie Times-News, p. 18; Drew Angerer/Getty Images, p. 19; David McNew/Getty Images, p. 20; Xinhua/Li Ying/Getty Images, p. 21; NOAA/Getty Images, p. 22; NASA/JPL, p. 23; ROBYN BECK/AFP/Getty Images, p. 24; Sky Noir Photography by Bill Dickinson/Moment/Getty Images, p. 25; Robert Nickelsberg/Getty Images, p. 26; ake1150sb/iStock/Getty Images, p. 27.

Cover: Jim Edds/Science Source/Getty Images.